IN-LINE SKATING

SKATING

BY JACK DAVID

TORQUE

BELLWETHER MEDIA • MINNEAPOLIS, MN

TORQUE™

Are you ready to take it to the extreme? Torque books thrust you into the action-packed world of sports, vehicles, and adventure. These books may include dirt, smoke, fire, and dangerous stunts. WARNING: Read at your own risk.

This edition first published in 2008 by Bellwether Media.

No part of this publication may be reproduced in whole or in part without written permission of the publisher. For information regarding permission, write to Bellwether Media Inc., Attention: Permissions Department, Post Office Box 19349, Minneapolis, MN 55419

Library of Congress Cataloging-in-Publication Data

David, Jack, 1968-
  In-line skating / by Jack David.
      p. cm. -- (Torque : action sports)
  Summary: "Amazing photography accompanies engaging information about In-Line skating. The combination of high-interest subject matter and light text is intended for students in grades 3 through 7"--Provided by publisher.
  Includes bibliographical references and index.
  ISBN-13: 978-1-60014-137-9 (hardcover : alk. paper)
  ISBN-10: 1-60014-137-4 (hardcover : alk. paper)
  1. In-line skating--Juvenile literature. I. Title.

  GV859.73.D38 2008
  796.21--dc22

                                                                2007042404

Schol. 8/09

CONTENTS

WHAT IS IN-LINE SKATING?

In-line skating is a great way to exercise and get around town. It can also be an extreme sport that pushes skaters to their limits.

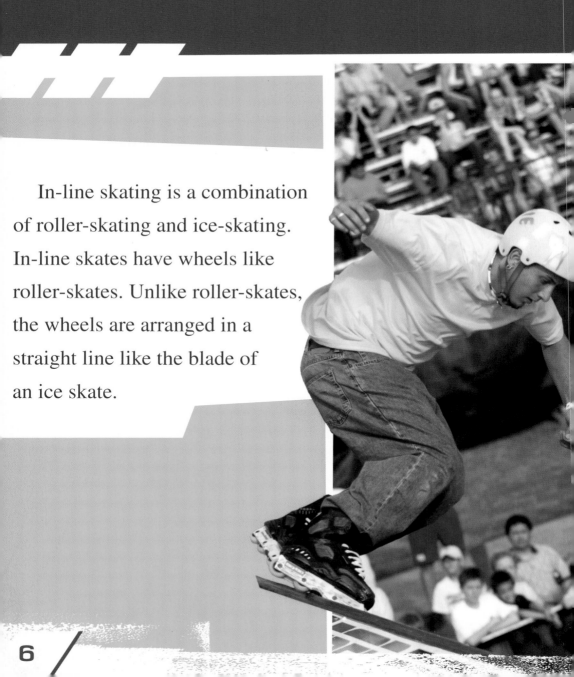

In-line skating is a combination of roller-skating and ice-skating. In-line skates have wheels like roller-skates. Unlike roller-skates, the wheels are arranged in a straight line like the blade of an ice skate.

Aggressive skating is the form of the sport that takes it to extremes. Aggressive skaters do jumps, **grabs**, and other stunts. Many show off their skills at skate parks. They jump off curved ramps. Some perform in U-shaped ramps called **half-pipes** or **vert ramps**.

IN-LINE SKATING EQUIPMENT

All in-line skates share some basic features. They include four or five wheels made of a hard plastic called **polyurethane**. A soft **liner** inside the skate cushions the foot. The liner is covered by a hard **shell**. The **frame** of the skate connects the wheels to the shell.

Safety is important for all skaters. A fall at a high speed can injure knees, elbows, wrists, or even the head.

Good safety equipment is key to enjoying the sport. Most skaters wear helmets, wrist guards, elbow pads, and kneepads for protection. Many also wear gloves and even shin guards.

IN-LINE SKATING IN ACTION

Aggressive skating competitions feature amazing stunts. In vert events, skaters speed up a steep vert ramp. They fly above the ramp's top edge. They spin, flip, and do other daring tricks while soaring through the air. They can also do tricks such as handstands on the ramp's edge. Skaters always try for a solid landing back on the ramp and a smooth ride back down. Judges score the tricks to decide the winner.

In street events, skaters compete on a street course. They use the natural features of the street for their tricks. Skaters pack in as many daring tricks as they can in a certain amount of time. They may jump off ledges or stairs and even leap over benches. Competitions may also have special ramps and rails set up to challenge skaters. A **grind** is a popular stunt for street skaters. The skater rides down a railing with the skates turned sideways. He moves on a part of the skate's frame instead of on the wheels.

FaSt FaCt

Aggressive skaters use skates with grind plates. These pieces of metal or hard plastic protect the frame of the skate during grinds.

19

In-line speed skating is a popular type of racing. These races take place both indoors and outside. While racing indoors, speed skaters race around four columns set in a rectangular shape. Racers may also skate at top speed through city streets or through parks. Speed skaters skate in areas cleared of people and traffic as they sprint toward the finish line.

GLOSSARY

frame—the part of an in-line skate that connects the wheels to the shell

grab—a trick in which a skater grabs hold of part of his or her skate while in the air

grind—to move along an obstacle such as a railing with the skates turned sideways; a part of the skate's frame, instead of the wheels, moves along the railing.

half-pipe—a ramp with steep walls; a half-pipe looks like half of a round pipe.

liner—the soft, inside part of an in-line skate

polyurethane—a hard plastic used to make wheels for in-line skates

shell—the hard outer casing of an in-line skate

vert ramp—a half-pipe with sides that become vertical, or straight up and down, at the top

TO LEARN MORE

AT THE LIBRARY

Bizley, Kirk. *In-Line Skating*. Chicago, Ill.:
Heinemann, 2000.

Blomquist, Christopher. *In-Line Skating in the X
Games*. New York: PowerKids Press, 2003.

Crossingham, John. *Extreme In-Line Skating*.
New York: Crabtree, 2004.

ON THE WEB
Learning more about in-line skating
is as easy as 1, 2, 3.

1. Go to www.factsurfer.com
2. Enter "in-line skating" into search box.
3. Click the "Surf" button and you will see a list
   of related web sites.

With factsurfer.com, finding more
information is just a click away.

INDEX

The images in this book are reproduced through the courtesy of: ESPN Images, front cover, pp. 3, 6, 7, 8, 9, 11, 13, 14, 15, 16-17, 18, 19, 21 (bottom); Stanley Chou/Getty Images, pp. 4-5; Juan Martinez, pp 10, 12; Cathrin Mueller/Bongarts/Getty Images, pp. 20, 21 (top).

DATE DUE

DEMCO, INC. 38-2931